KT-163-810

Contents

Welcome to France

France is the largest country in Europe. Its borders roughly follow the shape of a hexagon. At its north-western edge is the English Channel; to the west is the Atlantic Ocean.

The Mediterranean Sea forms the south-east border and the mountains of the Pyrénées are France's south-west limit. Mountains – the Alps and the Jura – also make up most of the eastern border. It is only to the north-east that the border between France and neighbouring countries is flat, low-lying land. The island of Corsica, roughly 180 kilometres south-east of France, is also French territory.

Worldwide popularity and reputation

France has a variety of landscapes, including low-lying wetlands and high mountain ranges. There are many historic towns, such as Chartres, Orléans and Reims, and chateaux (castles) like those in the Loire valley, which attract tourists. The capital city is Paris, famous for the Louvre museum and Notre Dame cathedral.

France is known worldwide for the food it produces, in particular its wine and cheese. The French have a reputation for being gourmets (a French word that means people who enjoy good food).

▲ The village of Huez in the Alps is snowbound in winter.

Fields and farmhouses near Rouen in northern France. ▼

GREAT BRITAIN

Capital ◻
Major cities and towns ○
Mountains
Grassland and farming
Country boundary

| 0 | | | 150 Miles |
| 0 | | | 250 Kilometres |

NORTH SEA

NETHERLANDS

BELGIUM

GERMANY

50°N

ENGLISH CHANNEL

Dunkerque
Calais
Boulogne
Lille

LUXEMBOURG

Dieppe

Cherbourg

Guernsey
CHANNEL ISLANDS
Jersey

N O R M A N D Y

Rouen

Seine

Reims

Marne

Metz

Meuse

Nancy

Strasbourg

St.-Malo

Caen

Versaille
PARIS

VOSGES

Brest
B R I T T A N Y

Quimper

Chartre

Seine

Le Mans

Orléans

Saône

Dijon

Moselle

Nantes
Anger
Saumu

Tours

F R A N C E

Loire

JURA

SWITZERLAND

Poitiers

ATLANTIC

La Rochelle

Bay of Biscay

OCEAN

Limoges

Saône

Lyons

Loire

Rhône

Chamoni
Mont Blanc

A L P S

ITALY

M A S S I F
A U V E R G N E
C E N T R A L

Dordogne

Bordeaux

Lot

Rhône

P R O V E N C E

Garonne

Monte Carlo
Nice

CORSICA

Biarritz

Toulouse

Montpellie

Cannes

Marseilles

St.Tropez

Bastia

Lourdes

Toulon

P Y R E N É E S

ANDORRA

M E D I T E R R A N E A N   S E A

Ajaccio

SPAIN

N
W   E
S

The Land

France has a varied landscape, with many different natural features. The climate is mainly temperate but other conditions are found in, for example, the coastal and mountainous regions.

Across France there are rivers, lakes, salt marshes and gentle hills as well as mountains, flat plains and coasts. Over half of France is low-lying but there are also spectacular mountainous areas to the south and east. The highest peak in Europe, Mont Blanc, is in the French Alps.

Central France is characterised by an area of extinct volcanoes called the Massif Central.

Large rivers

France has four main rivers, the longest of which is the Loire. The River Seine flows through Paris, while in the south the River Garonne has cut deep gorges into the land. The Rhône, to the east, has formed a delta where it flows into the Mediterranean Sea.

Animals and Plants

Different areas of France are home to different types of animals and plants, for example:
- Chamois deer live in the Alps
- wild boar are found in forests in the north
- oak forests grow in the north and west
- in the south there are olive trees and herbs such as thyme and rosemary.

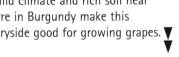
The mild climate and rich soil near Auxerre in Burgundy make this countryside good for growing grapes. ▼

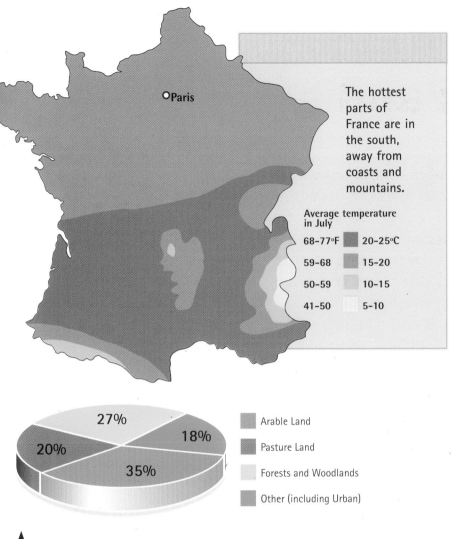

The hottest parts of France are in the south, away from coasts and mountains.

Average temperature in July

68–77°F	20–25°C
59–68	15–20
50–59	10–15
41–50	5–10

Arable Land

Pasture Land

Forests and Woodlands

Other (including Urban)

▲ How the land is used.

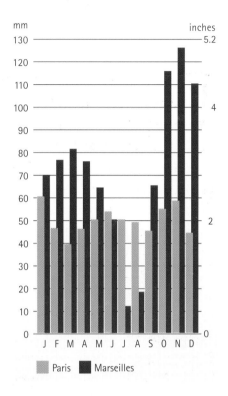

Paris ■ Marseilles

▲▲ A comparison of the monthly rainfall of two major cities in France.

Climate

Most of France has mild winters and warm summers. This is called a temperate climate. However, mountainous areas, such as the Alps, have much colder winters which can bring heavy snow falls.

The south, next to the Mediterranean Sea, has the hottest, driest summers and warmest winters in France. This is called a Mediterranean climate. Rain falls mainly in the autumn and winter.

Another feature of the climate in the south is the Mistral, a cold wind that blows down the Rhône valley at certain times of the year. It sometimes blows hard enough to damage whole fields of crops.

Web Search ▶▶

▶ http://www.abritel.fr/uk/meteo24.php
Today's weather and forecast for France.

▶ http://www.meteofrance.com/FR/index.jsp
Weather and climate for France.

▶ http://www.franceguide.com
General information about France, including maps, travel and tourist sites.

The People

With fewer babies being born and people living longer, France now has a very slow-growing, ageing population. The people making up the French nation have many different origins. A shared official language helps to build a sense of national identity.

The population of France is just over 60 million. At present it is growing at 0.3–0.4 per cent a year. This is because people are choosing to have small families with only one or two children. As a result the percentage of elderly people in France is increasing, while the percentage of population under 15 years is diminishing.

A population of mixed origins

Most modern French people are descended from the Celtic Gauls, who moved into what is now France from 1500 to 500 BC, from the Romans, and from the Franks, a group of West Germanic people who took over the region from about AD 500. More recently there have also been immigrants from the Middle East, Portugal, Russia, Southeast Asia and North Africa.

▲ Inside the Galeries Lafayette department store in Paris. French people and tourists shop here for all kinds of goods.

Changes in population since 1970. Overall, the population is getting older. In 1970, 67% of people were aged over 20; in 2004, the figure was 77%. ▼

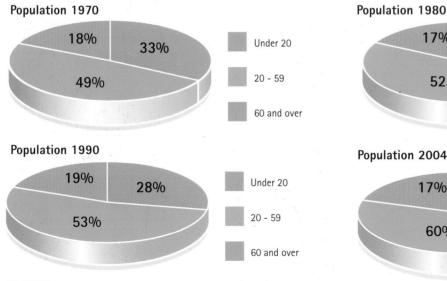

Population 1970
18%
33%
49%
- Under 20
- 20 - 59
- 60 and over

Population 1980
17%
30.5%
52.5%
- Under 20
- 20 - 59
- 60 and over

Population 1990
19%
28%
53%
- Under 20
- 20 - 59
- 60 and over

Population 2004
17%
23%
60%
- Under 20
- 20 - 59
- 60 and over

A common language

French is the official national language. It mainly grew out of Latin, the language of the Romans. Some areas in France have kept traditional languages – Flemish in the far north, Breton in Brittany, Basque and Catalan in the areas bordering Spain, and Provençal in Provence.

French is also an official language in Belgium, Switzerland, Luxembourg, Canada and more than 30 countries in Africa, the Caribbean and the Pacific islands that formed part of the French colonial empire. Altogether, about 200 million people in the world speak French.

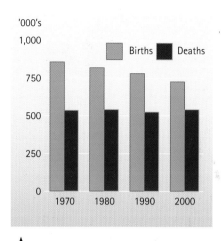

▲ Changes in numbers of births and deaths in France since 1970.

◄◄ Artists from all over the world sit and paint in the Montmartre district of Paris. Situated in the shadow of the Sacre-Coeur, one of the city's oldest churches, the area is filled with traditional French restaurants.

Web Search ►►

► http://www.paris.org
A guide to Paris, the capital city.

► http://www.info-france-usa.org/kids/
All about France for children.

► http://www.brittany-bretagne.com
Guide to the north-west of France, the Breton region.

► http://www.odci.gov/cia/publications/factbook/geos/fr.html
The US Central Intelligence Agency factbook on France, including maps.

Urban and Rural Life

The population of France is spread very unevenly throughout the country. Over the past 50 years more people have moved to urban areas. This is largely because of the higher number of job opportunities available when compared to rural areas.

Mountainous regions, such as the Pyrénées, have less than 15 people per square kilometre because it is very hard to make a living there. People choose to live in low-lying parts of the country, such as the area around Paris, because it is easier to farm and build on the land. The area around Paris has over 150 people per square kilometre.

There has been a big shift in population from the countryside to cities since World War II. By 2005 France had 45 million people living in towns and cities. The largest cities include Paris, Marseilles and Lyons.

Many villages in France, like this one in Normandy, lie among hills and are surrounded by farmland and trees. ▼

People on the move

Urban areas offer more job opportunities in offices, shops and banks. People are also moving to some areas because they have a pleasant climate, for example the area along the Mediterranean coast.

People in urban areas have traditionally lived in apartments situated in large old buildings around the town or city centre. After World War II, there was a housing shortage and so modern, high-rise flats were built on the edges of large urban areas. Those people that could afford to began to move to detached houses in the suburbs.

Renting farmhouses, building new homes

In isolated rural areas, farmhouses have been left empty as people have moved into towns. In parts of Brittany and the Massif Central some farmers have started renting out these farmhouses to tourists and have used the money to build new houses for themselves.

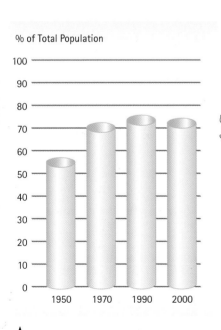

▲ A view over Paris, the largest and most populated city in France. To the right of centre stands the Eiffel Tower.

% of Total Population

▲ How the urban population has changed since 1950.

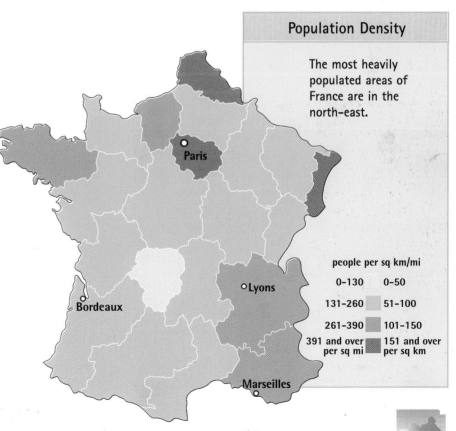

Population Density

The most heavily populated areas of France are in the north-east.

people per sq km/mi

0–130	0–50
131–260	51–100
261–390	101–150
391 and over per sq mi	151 and over per sq km

▲
▲ A fisherman returns to harbour with his catch of crabs.

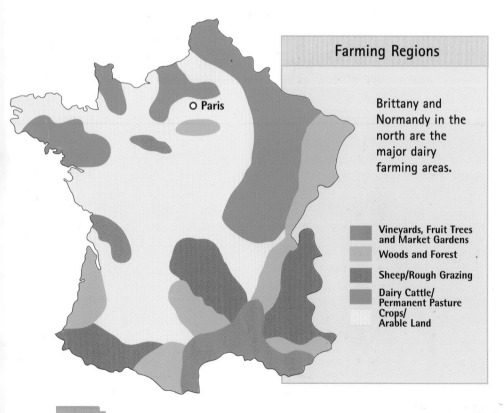

Farming Regions

O Paris

Brittany and
Normandy in the
north are the
major dairy
farming areas.

Vineyards, Fruit Trees
and Market Gardens

Woods and Forest

Sheep/Rough Grazing

Dairy Cattle/
Permanent Pasture
Crops/
Arable Land

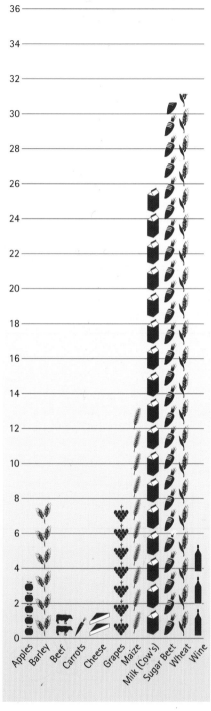

Million Tonnes

36

34

32

30

28

26

24

22

20

18

16

14

12

10

8

6

4

2

0

Apples · Barley · Beef · Carrots · Cheese · Grapes · Maize · Milk (Cow's) · Sugar Beet · Wheat · Wine

▲
▲ Main farming products. France
ranks in the world's top 10 producers of
meat, milk and various fruits and
vegetables.

Farming and Fishing

E ven though farming and fishing provide the French population with most of what they need to eat, these industries do not employ many people. Nevertheless, farmers contribute to the French economy by producing goods for the export market.

Over half of the land in France is used for farming. Wheat and corn are grown where land is low-lying and the climate is cooler and wetter. Cattle, reared for milk and beef, are found in many regions, except the area around the Mediterranean where it is too hot. Sheep are found mainly in mountainous areas. Grape vines and fruit, such as peaches and lemons, are grown mainly in the warmer, more southern areas.

Fishing

Fishing is an important economic activity in the coastal regions of France. As well as the main ports such as Cherbourg and Quimper, there are small fishing boats operating from most coastal villages.

Fishing boats from France work around the coast of Europe, Iceland, the east coast of Canada and the west coast of Africa.

The French eat about 30 kilograms of fish a year per person, compared to 20 kilograms in the UK.

Changes in farming

In the past farming was especially important to France because the economy was based on agriculture. Today, only four per cent of the workforce are farmers.

However, because France is able to grow more food than it needs and can sell the surplus to other countries, farming is still an important industry for the nation.

France is the second largest food exporter in the world. In the 1940s, one farmer could grow enough food to feed five people. By 2000, one farmer could feed more than 30 people. This is because many farms have become bigger and use more machinery, fertilizers and pesticides. In the more remote rural areas, farms are still small and farming methods are more traditional.

◄◄ Farmers pick grapes from a vineyard near Cahors, south-west France.

Resources and Industry

The natural resources of France were once used to provide energy and raw materials for French manufacturing industries. Nowadays it is cheaper to import such resources. Many manufacturing industries no longer employ as many people as in the past; service industries now provide most jobs.

Until the 1960s most of France's energy supply came from coal mined in the north. When this began to run out, oil and gas were used, although most of this had to be imported. Today, electricity is mainly supplied by nuclear power stations; they produce over 80 per cent of France's energy needs. Hydroelectric power is produced, using the fast-flowing rivers of mountainous areas such as the Alps. There is also a tidal power station at Rance in Normandy, and wind power stations in Brittany.

Employment by type of industry. ▼▼

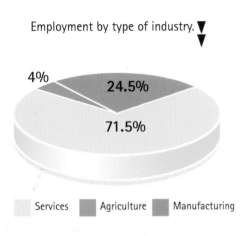

4%
24.5%
71.5%

☐ Services ▨ Agriculture ▧ Manufacturing

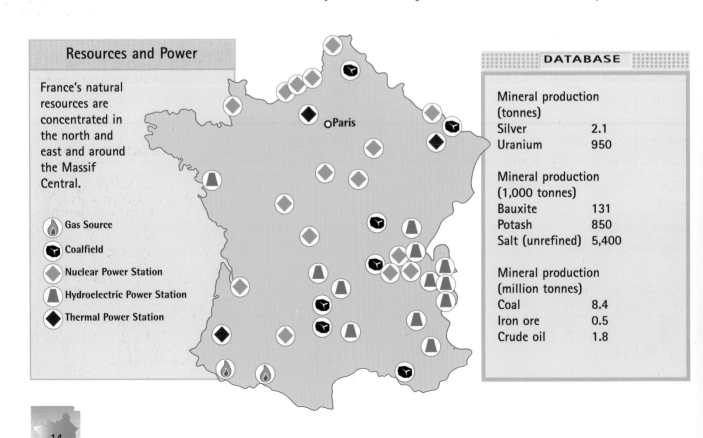

Resources and Power

France's natural resources are concentrated in the north and east and around the Massif Central.

- ⬤ Gas Source
- ⬤ Coalfield
- ◆ Nuclear Power Station
- ⬤ Hydroelectric Power Station
- ◆ Thermal Power Station

○Paris

DATABASE

Mineral production
(tonnes)
Silver   2.1
Uranium   950

Mineral production
(1,000 tonnes)
Bauxite   131
Potash   850
Salt (unrefined) 5,400

Mineral production
(million tonnes)
Coal   8.4
Iron ore   0.5
Crude oil   1.8

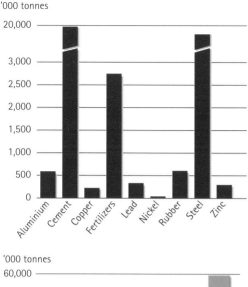

'000 tonnes

(Bar chart: Aluminium, Cement, Copper, Fertilizers, Lead, Nickel, Rubber, Steel, Zinc)

'000 tonnes

(Bar chart: Cars, Commercial Vehicles, Radios, TVs, Tyres)

◄◄ Quantities of materials and manufactured goods produced by French industry.

▲ A tanker ship fills up at an oil refinery at Le Havre in northern France.

Manufacturing and mining

Smelting and shipbuilding are still major industries. Minerals mined on a small scale in north-west France include bauxite (used to produce aluminium), potash and sodium chloride (salt).

The car and electronics industries are important for France's economy. Companies such as Citroën, Renault and the electronics corporation, Thomson Multimedia, sell their products internationally. The French aircraft and aerospace industries are also respected worldwide.

Service industries

The main growth areas of the French service industries are in the insurance, advertising, telecommunication, hotel and information technology sectors. France is a world leader in biotechnology, robotics and medicine.

Web Search ►►

► http://www.cenerg.cma.fr
Information from France's Centre for Energy Studies.

► http://www.minefi.gouv.fr
Website of the Ministry of Economy, Finance and Industry.

► http://www.cea.fr/default_gb.htm
Information from France's atomic energy authority.

Transport

Getting Around in Paris

THE METRO: this is the underground rail network. No point in Paris is more than 500m from an underground station. It is quick, efficient and easy to use.

BUSES: there is an extensive network of bus routes, but the heavy traffic in Paris can mean slow journeys.

TAXIS: these can be flagged down anywhere or found at taxi stands.

RIVER TAXIS (boats): during the summer a shuttle service stops at the main tourist sites on or near the River Seine in Paris.

All the road, rail and air networks in France carry a large number of passengers and great quantities of freight. There are also strong transport links with other countries by road, rail, air and sea.

France has a large motorway (autoroute) network. On some autoroutes drivers have to pay money – called 'tolls' – to use them. There is also a network of main roads and smaller roads. Road transport is used widely to carry both passengers and freight.

The rail network is made up of main lines radiating out from Paris. These include special tracks for the high-speed train system called the Train à Grande Vitesse (TGV). Travelling by TGV is often faster than going by air. Air travel is important within France because of the size of the country. Airports furthest away from Paris are particularly busy because of this. For example, Nice airport handles more than 6 million passengers a year.

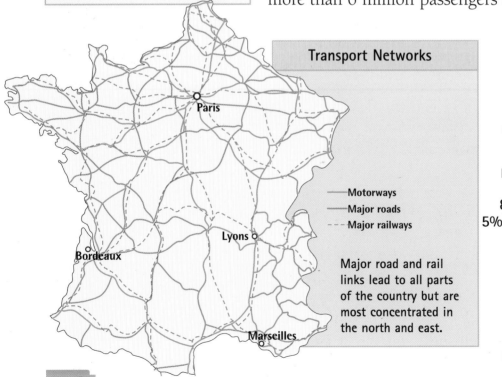

Transport Networks

—— Motorways
—— Major roads
- - - Major railways

Major road and rail links lead to all parts of the country but are most concentrated in the north and east.

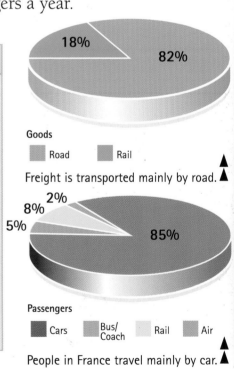

Goods

■ Road   ■ Rail

Freight is transported mainly by road. ▲

Passengers

■ Cars   ■ Bus/Coach   ■ Rail   ■ Air

People in France travel mainly by car. ▲

▲ The Eurostar train takes passengers from London to Paris through the Channel Tunnel. A TGV train tunnel is now being built through the Pyrénées to link southern France and Spain.

◄◄ Travellers emerge from the Métro, the underground railway of Paris.

🌐 **Web Search** ►►

► http://www.smartweb.fr/
   aero/index.html
   Details of Paris airports and flights.

► http://www.sncf.com/
   indexe.htm
   French railways.

► http://about-france.com
   Travel to and around France.

Links with other countries

France's road and rail networks are linked to the rest of Europe. The Mont Blanc road tunnel links France and Italy. The Channel Tunnel links France and England. There are international airports in many of the larger towns. Sea ferry services run from French ports to England, Ireland, Spain, North Africa and Sardinia.

▲ Every school in France and in the overseas French colonies has a similar curriculum. Children increasingly use computers in school.

▶▶ Many small villages in France have a local school where children of very different ages attend classes. The children are taught several subjects by the same teacher.

18

Education

I n France, education can be public or private. Most children go to public schools that are run by the Ministry of National Education.

Education is free for all children aged 6 to 16. It is also compulsory, meaning that all children in this age range must go to school. Some children go to nursery schools when they are 2 years old. Children attend primary schools between the ages of 6 and 11. After primary school they go to the local secondary school until they are 15 or 16, when they choose whether they want to continue studying or leave school and train for a job.

The baccalauréat

Students study a wide range of subjects. When they are 16, they can choose to concentrate on languages, economics or science, but they also continue with other subjects. When they are 18, students can take the university entrance exam, called the general baccalauréat. If they pass, they may go to one of the 77 universities in France.

Students who leave school at 16 may go to a technical college to learn a skill that will help them get a job. In all schools, children do not have to wear school uniforms.

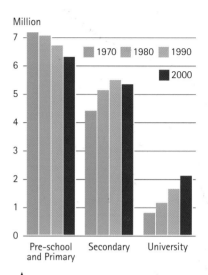

▲ Numbers of pupils in each category of education (1,000).

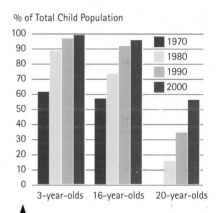

▲ Percentage of selected age groups who enrolled in education.

Term-time and holidays

Most primary- and some secondary-school children in France go to school on Saturday mornings. There are no lessons on Wednesday afternoons. This time is used for sports.

The summer holiday lasts nine weeks, which is longer than in most other European countries. However, in term-time the school day is long and a lot of homework is set.

Web Search ►►

► http://www.education.fr
Details of education in France.

► http://www.frenchentree.com/fe-education/
Site of the French Ministry of Education.

Sport and Leisure

Nowadays, more than ever before, French people have money and time to pursue leisure interests. About 70 per cent of families take a holiday at least once a year. Most of these holidays are taken in France. Watching and playing sports is also very popular.

The French enjoy sports such as soccer, rugby, tennis, basketball, motor racing, skiing and cycling. Soccer has become even more popular after the national team won the World Cup and the European Cup. A number of famous sporting events take place every year, for example, the French Open Tennis Championship and the Tour de France cycle race.

▶▶ The Tour de France race leaders. The cyclists are followed by race supervisors, police and television camera operators on motorcycles.

Outdoor activities

Watersports, such as swimming and diving, are very popular both in the sea and on inland lakes such as Lac d'Annecy in the Alps. Mountains, such as the Alps and the Pyrénées, offer the chance to ski and snowboard in the winter and to hike in the summer.

French people enjoy taking long holidays in the summer. Families stay at seaside resorts or in gîtes (rented holiday homes) in the countryside in France. Tourism has become a very important industry, providing many jobs and valuable income for local rural economies. About 70 million tourists come to France every year from abroad, using its hotels, restaurants and visiting tourist attractions such as EuroDisney near Paris. Since 1980 the amount of money tourists spend in France has increased dramatically.

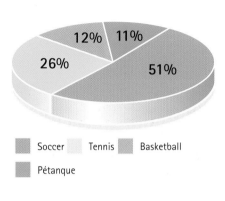

Soccer   Tennis   Basketball   Pétanque

▲ Numbers of sports clubs. Pétanque is a type of bowls played with metal balls.

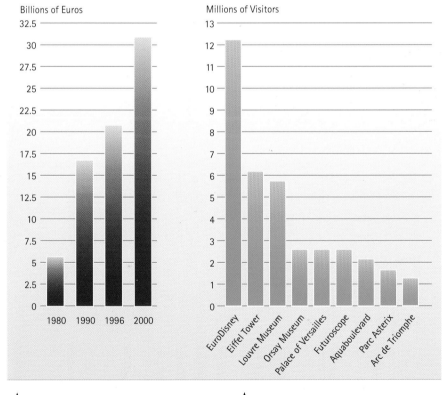

▲ Growth in money spent by tourists in France, in billions of euros.

▲ Most popular tourist sites in France – millions of visitors each year.

Web Search ▶▶

▶ http://www.tifonet.it/soccer
Pictures from 1998 when France won the World Cup final.

▶ http://www.cyclingnews.com
Tour de France and other cycling news.

▶ http://www.france-online.usa.sa.com
Tourist information for France.

▶ http://www.francetourism.com
French Tourist Office.

▶ http://www.paris.org
Tourist information about Paris.

Daily Life and Religion

French people come from a variety of religious and cultural backgrounds. They spend almost eight per cent of their income on eating out in restaurants.

The French work an average of 39 hours a week. Daily working hours are from about 8 a.m. until 6 p.m., often with a 2-hour lunch break. Most offices, construction sites and factories are closed at weekends.

Shops

French people buy goods at a range of retail outlets. There are small shops selling particular kinds of food, for instance charcuteries that sell cooked meats and boulangeries that sell bread. There are also hypermarchés (enormous supermarkets) selling all types of food and drink as well as clothes and household equipment. The small shops are found in villages and in town centres; hypermarchés are usually built on the outskirts of town. Most towns also have a weekly street market.

Armed forces

France's armed forces total 347,000 professional troops, divided into land, air and sea forces. There is also a police force, called the gendarmerie, which is part of the armed forces.

In 2005, 34,000 French troops were based overseas. Some of them formed part of international peace-keeping and aid distribution forces.

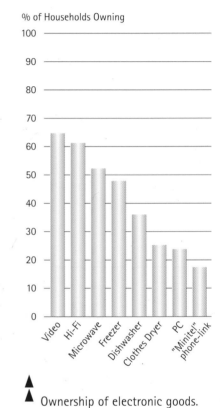

% of Households Owning

Ownership of electronic goods.

Notre Dame in Paris, one of the most famous churches in France. ▼

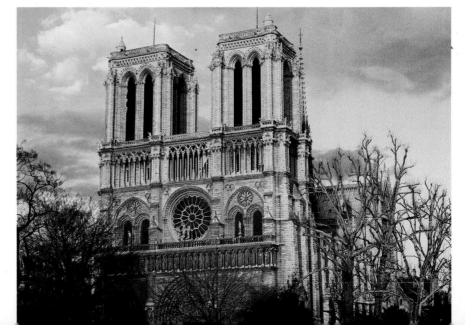

◄◄ Fruit for sale at a street market in France.

Web Search ►►

► http://www.sante.gouv.fr
General health information.

► http://www.defense.gouv.fr
Website of the Ministry of Defence.

► http://www.info-europe.fr
The European Union website for all aspects of French life.

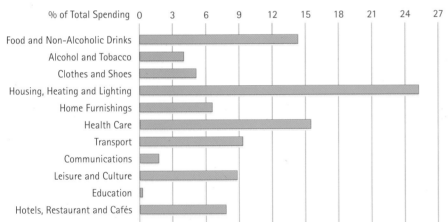

% of Total Spending	
Food and Non-Alcoholic Drinks	
Alcohol and Tobacco	
Clothes and Shoes	
Housing, Heating and Lighting	
Home Furnishings	
Health Care	
Transport	
Communications	
Leisure and Culture	
Education	
Hotels, Restaurant and Cafés	

◄◄ How French households spend their money. The cost of living in France is high compared to many non-European countries, but in Europe it is not much above average.

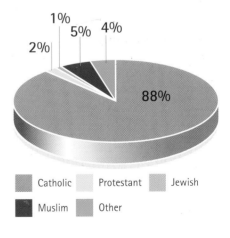

1%   5%   4%
2%
88%

Catholic   Protestant   Jewish
Muslim   Other

▲
▲ Different religions in France.

Religion

There is no official state religion in France. About 88 per cent of the French population say they are Roman Catholic, but many of them do not go to church. The second largest religious group follow the Islamic faith: there are over 3 million Muslims in France; many of them immigrants or children of immigrants from North Africa. There are also about 1 million Protestants and about 500,000 Jews.

Arts and Media

People are attracted to the chateaux, cathedrals and palaces in France – this is the Palais Longchamp, Marseilles. ▼

France possesses some of the world's most famous museums and art galleries. It is also renowned for its cultural events, including the annual film festival at Cannes in southern France.

Some of the best known art galleries are found in Paris, including the Louvre and the Pompidou Centre of Art and Culture. Over the years, many French artists have become known throughout the world, for example the Impressionists including Claude Monet and Auguste Renoir. France has also produced several of the world's greatest writers, philosophers, singers and composers of classical music.

Going to see films has been a popular leisure activity in France ever since the opening of the world's first public cinema in Paris, in 1895. Even today, cinema audiences are higher than in other European countries. In 1987, a unique theme park about cinema, video and visual technology, called Futuroscope, was opened near Poitiers.

◄◄ These unusual structures form part of the fountain outside the Pompidou Centre in Paris.

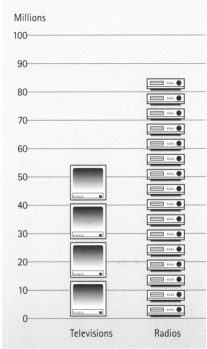

Millions

100	
90	
80	
70	
60	
50	
40	
30	
20	
10	
0	
Televisions	Radios

▲ Ownership of televisions and radios.

The national press

Daily newspapers are published in about 40 French cities and more than 12 in Paris itself. Two of the daily national papers, *Le Monde* and *Le Figaro*, are world famous. There are also daily regional papers, for example *Ouest-France*, which sells more copies in France every day than any other paper. As well as newspapers there are magazines, such as *Paris-Match* and *Elle*.

Television and radio

With 116 channels, including cable and pay-TV, French TV viewers have plenty to choose from. The average time spent watching television is 16 hours per week. There are hundreds of radio broadcast stations. Most are local commercial stations that broadcast not only in French but in English and other European languages.

Web Search ►►

► http://www.lemonde.fr
Read the French newspaper Le Monde.

► http://www.cplus.fr
Television viewing details from Canal+ broadcast station.

► http://www.paris.org/ Musees
Details of museums in Paris.

► http://www.futuroscope.fr
Website of Futuroscope theme park.

► http://www.louvre.fr
View the collection of the Louvre museum in Paris.

▲ The Government office building in the town of Nancy in north-east France. The office deals with law and order for local and overseas départements.

French overseas départements.

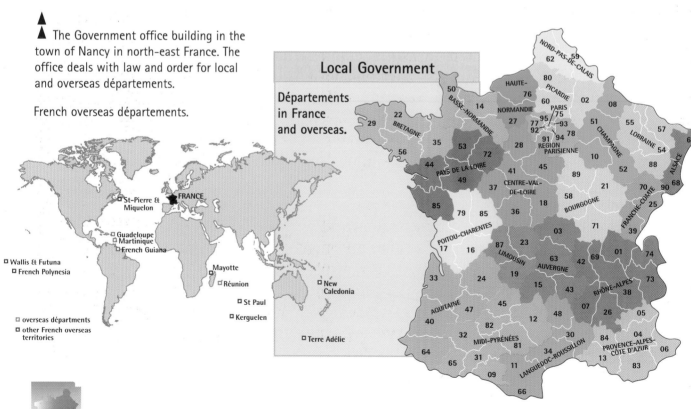

Local Government

Départements
in France
and overseas.

St-Pierre & Miquelon
★ FRANCE

Guadeloupe
Martinique
French Guiana

Wallis & Futuna
French Polynesia

Mayotte
Réunion

New Caledonia

St Paul
Kerguelen

□ overseas départements
□ other French overseas territories

Terre Adélie

NORD-PAS-DE-CALAIS 59
62
80
HAUTE-NORMANDIE 76
50
14
BASSE-NORMANDIE
22
29 BRETAGNE
PICARDIE 60 02 08
PARIS 75
95 77 93
92 94 78
91 REGION PARISIENNE
51 55 57
CHAMPAGNE LORRAINE 54
88 ALSACE 67
27
35 53 72
28
44 PAYS DE LA LOIRE 49
41 45
37 CENTRE-VAL-DE-LOIRE
10
89 52
21 58 BOURGOGNE
70 90 68
FRANCHE-COMTÉ 25
56
85 79 85 36 18
71 39
POITOU-CHARENTES 03
17 16 87 23
LIMOUSIN 63 AUVERGNE 42 69 01 74
33 24 19 15 43 RHÔNE-ALPES 38 73
AQUITAINE 47 45 48 07 26 05
40 82 12 30 84 PROVENCE-ALPES-CÔTE D'AZUR 06
32 MIDI-PYRÉNÉES 81 34 LANGUEDOC-ROUSSILLON 13 83
64 31 11
65 09 66

Government

France is a democracy in which the people elect members of the National Assembly and Senate, which together make up Parliament.

France does not have a royal family; it became a republic in 1789. The President is the head of state and appoints the Prime Minister. The President of the Republic is elected for seven years.

The National Assembly has 577 deputies elected by the people for five years. The Senate has 321 senators elected by local councillors and the National Assembly for nine years. The President has the power to make the major decisions but needs support from the Prime Minister and Parliament. If the President and Prime Minister are from different political parties, this can lead to conflict.

Political parties

The main political parties are the Socialist Party, the Communist Party, the Republican Party, and the Democratic Union. There are also regional and local governments. France is divided into 22 regions. Each region is divided into areas called départements. There are 96 of these in mainland France and 5 overseas. Each département has a council elected by the residents. These councils have the power to make local decisions.

Overseas départements

Départements such as Guadaloupe in the West Indies have the same rights as those in France. Each has a Regional Council that makes local decisions and elects members to the French Parliament based in Paris. They are subject to French laws and have French schools, police and currency. In 2002 the euro replaced the French franc as the new national currency of France.

Département Names and Numbers

Most départements are named after geographical features, mainly rivers, for example Dordogne in the region of Aquitaine and Tarn in the Midi-Pyrénées.

Every département has a number. These are used on car registration plates. For example, number 75 is for the centre of Paris.

Web Search ▶▶

▶ http://www.french-at-a-touch.com/Countries/france.htm
Information on the regions and département.

▶ http://www.premier-ministre.gouv.fr/en
Website of France's Prime Minister.

▶ http://www.assemblee-nat.fr
Information about the National Assembly.

▶ http://www.tahiti.com
The island of Tahiti in French Polynesia.

Place in the World

France has played an important part in European history for over 1,500 years. Its role in the wider world began with the founding of colonies in North America in 1608 and continues into the 21st century.

France is a key member of the European Union (EU). In fact, the idea for the EU first came from France after World War II. The aim was to build friendship between France and Germany in order to prevent any more wars between the two countries.

As the EU has grown to include many members, France has continued to play a central role in it. France has the second largest economy in the EU and therefore contributes large sums of money to paying for the costs of building the union. Most French people like being members of the EU and support its policies and plans.

The present political system in France was set up in 1958 when Charles de Gaulle became President. Soon after, France was involved in fighting with Vietnam and Algeria, two of its colonies that wanted independence. By 1969 all its colonies had become independent countries. Today, France still has strong links with these countries.

9 May 1950 – at a meeting in Paris of foreign leaders, the French Foreign Minister reads out the terms for co-operation between European nations. This has become today's European Union. ▼

◄◄ At Kourou in French Guiana a nose cone containing satellites for European television companies is being taken to a launch pad to be loaded onto a rocket for transport into space. France plays a major role in the European Space Agency and its rocket site in French Guiana is used by many countries.

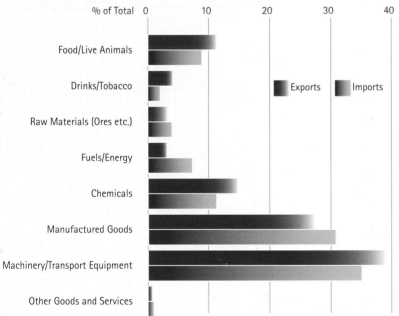

Web Search ►►

► http://www.franceway.com
French history.

► http://www.ambafrance-au.org
Information about France from a French Embassy.

► http://www.diplomatie.gouv.fr
French Ministry of Foreign Affairs.

► http://www.legifrance.gouv.fr
General information on the French constitution.

► http://www.euro.gouv.fr
French Ministry of Finance.

► http://www.europa.eu.int/index_en.htm
General information about the EU.

► http://www.premier-ministre.gouv.fr/en
The French Prime Minister.

◄◄ Comparative figures for France's imports and exports. Its major trading partners are other members of the EU.

29

Area:
547,026 sq km.

Population size:
60,424,000.

Capital city:
Paris (2,142,800).

Other major cities:
Marseilles, Lyons, Toulouse.

Longest river:
Loire (1,012km).

Highest mountain:
Mont Blanc (4,807m).

Largest lake:
Lac Léman (239sq km in France).

Flag:
Blue, white and red vertical stripes known as the tricolour. Dates from the French Revolution in 1789. Blue and red were the city colours of Paris where the revolution began. White was the old French royal colour.

Official language:
French.

Currency:
euro
1 euro = 100 euro cents.

Major resources:
Uranium, potash, salt, oil, iron ore.

Major exports:
Machinery/transport equipment (for example, cars, tyres, aircraft); manufactured goods (for example, TVs, radios, computers).

National holidays:
New Year's Day (1 January)
Easter (late March/early April)
May Day (1 May)
Victory Day, WWII (8 May)
Ascension Day: 40th day after Easter (May)

Pentecost: 7th Sunday after Easter (mid-May/mid-June)
Whit Monday (mid-May/mid-June)
Bastille Day (14 July)
Assumption Day (15 August)
All Saints' Day (1 November)
Remembrance Day (11 November)
Christmas (25 December).

Religions:
Roman Catholicism, Islam (Muslim), Protestantism, Judaism.

30

Glossary

AGEING POPULATION
A population in which the proportion of people over 60 years of age is increasing and the proportion of those under 15 is decreasing.

BACCALAUREAT
The exam taken by French school students of 18 to qualify for a place at university.

BASQUES
People who originate from and live in the south-west area of France and the north-west area of Spain around the Bay of Biscay.

BRETONS
People who originate from and live in the region of Brittany.

CLIMATE
The average weather conditions experienced in one area over a period of time.

COLONIES
Countries which were taken over and ruled by other countries.

DELTA
Name given to new land which is built up out of sand and silt deposited by a river as it flows into the sea.

EUROPEAN UNION (EU)
A grouping of European countries that all trade with each other on commonly agreed terms.

EXPORTS
Goods and services sold by one country to others.

EXTINCT VOLCANO
A volcano that will never erupt again.

EURO
The currency that the countries of the European Union have agreed they will use when trading with each other.

FREIGHT
Goods and products that are carried by lorries, trains and ships.

GORGE
A steep-sided, deep valley cut into rock by a river.

HIGH-TECHNOLOGY INDUSTRIES
Industries and businesses that make or use the latest technology.

IMMIGRANTS
People who move from one country to live in another.

IMPORTS
Goods and services bought by one country from others.

IMPRESSIONISTS
Group of French artists who achieved fame in France and abroad between the 1860s and 1880s.

MANUFACTURING INDUSTRIES
Industries that make products from raw materials.

NATURAL VEGETATION
Plants and trees that grow in an area when humans have not interfered.

POPULATION DENSITY
The number of people living in an area, for example, in 1sq km.

RAW MATERIALS
The original materials needed to make products; for example, iron ore is needed to make steel.

RESOURCES
Things that can be used; for example, coal can be used to make electricity.

RURAL
In the country.

SERVICE INDUSTRIES
Industries which provide a service to people rather than make products.

SUBURBS
Areas of housing in towns and cities between the centre and the countryside.

TEMPERATE CLIMATE
A climate that has mild winters and warm summers.

TRAIN A GRANDE VITESSE (TGV)
High-speed train developed in 1981 that travels at up to 300kph.

URBAN
In towns and cities.

Index